D1265597

Salamanders

Leo Statts

abdopublishing.com

Published by Abdo Zoom™, PO Box 398166, Minneapolis, Minnesota 55439. Copyright © 2017 by Abdo Consulting Group, Inc. International copyrights reserved in all countries. No part of this book may be reproduced in any form without written permission from the publisher. Abdo Zoom™ is a trademark and logo of Abdo Consulting Group, Inc.

Printed in the United States of America, North Mankato, Minnesota
062016
092016

THIS BOOK CONTAINS
RECYCLED MATERIALS

Cover Photo: Shutterstock Images
Interior Photos: iStockphoto, 1, 6–7, 9, 10–11, 13, 16, 18; Jason Ondreicka/iStockphoto, 4–5, 8, 12–13; Shutterstock Images, 7; Red Line Editorial, 11, 20 (left), 20 (right), 21 (left), 21 (right); Rui Manuel Teles Gomes/Shutterstock Images, 14; Matt Jeppson/Shutterstock Images, 15; Robert Pavsic/iStockphoto, 19

Editor: Brienna Rossiter
Series Designer: Madeline Berger
Art Direction: Dorothy Toth

Publisher's Cataloging-in-Publication Data
Names: Statts, Leo, author.
Title: Salamanders / by Leo Statts.
Description: Minneapolis, MN : Abdo Zoom, [2017] | Series: Swamp animals |
    Includes bibliographical references and index.
Identifiers: LCCN 2016941193 | ISBN 9781680792119 (lib. bdg.) |
    ISBN 9781680793796 (ebook) | ISBN 9781680794687 (Read-to-me ebook)
Subjects: LCSH: Salamanders--Juvenile literature.
Classification: DDC 597.8--dc23
LC record available at http://lccn.loc.gov/2016941193

Table of Contents

Salamanders

Salamanders are amphibians. They have long tails. Their legs are short. If they lose a leg, they can grow it back.

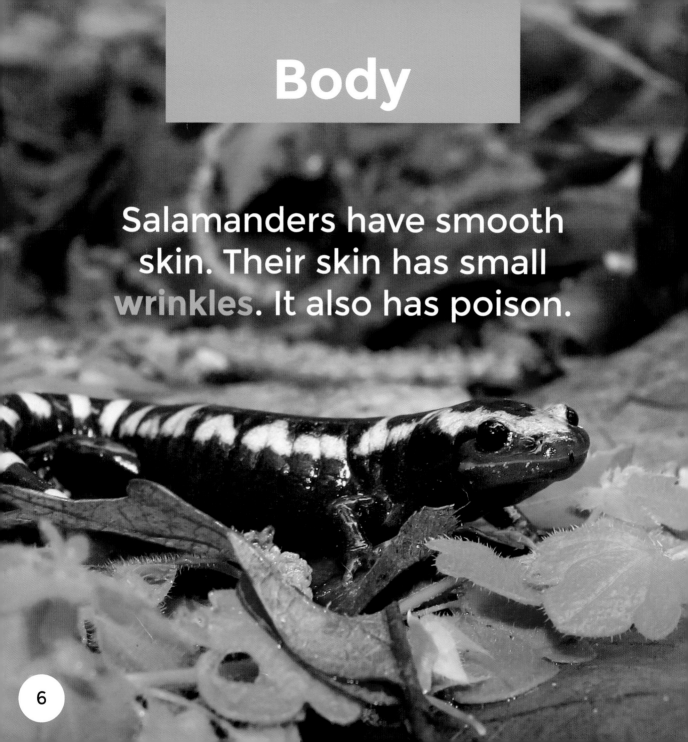

Body

Salamanders have smooth skin. Their skin has small **wrinkles**. It also has poison.

This helps them avoid being eaten by other animals.

Some salamanders have spots.
Others have stripes.

Some do not have lungs.
They breathe through their skin.

Habitat

Salamanders live all over the world. Some salamanders spend most of their lives in the water. Others live mostly on land.

Where salamanders live

Salamanders live in cool, wet places. Some hide under rocks or logs.

Others live in **burrows**.

Food

Salamanders eat insects.
Some even eat baby snakes.

They eat worms and mice, too.

Salamanders hide from their **prey**. Then they jump out. They catch the prey with their sticky tongues.

Life Cycle

Salamanders live about 10 years. Most lay eggs. **Larvae** later **hatch** from the eggs.

Other salamanders have live babies. The babies look like small adults.

Average Length – Shortest

A Mexican pygmy salamander is almost as long as a penny.

0.7 in   0.75 in

Average Length – Longest

A Chinese giant salamander is longer than an acoustic guitar.

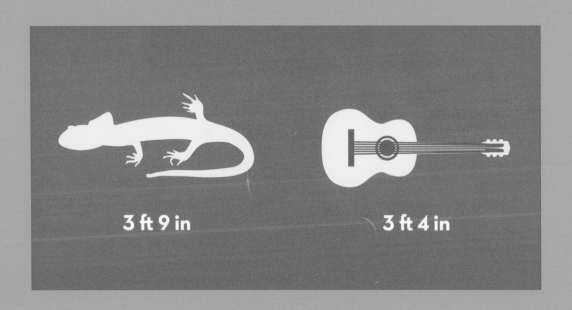

3 ft 9 in   3 ft 4 in

Glossary

amphibian - a cold-blooded animal that can live in water and on land.

burrow - an animal's underground home.

hatch - to be born from an egg.

larvae - animals in a very young form.

prey - an animal that is hunted and eaten by another animal.

wrinkles - lines or folds in the skin.

Booklinks

For more information
on salamanders, please visit
booklinks.abdopublishing.com

Zoom In on Animals!

Learn even more with the Abdo Zoom
Animals database. Check out
abdozoom.com for more information.

Index